THE FIRST
Settlements

by
LINDA THOMPSON

Rourke
Publishing LLC
Vero Beach, Florida 32964

www.rourkepublishing.com

PHOTO CREDITS:
Courtesy CA Department of Conservation, CA Geological Survey: page 9; Courtesy Historical Society of Pennsylvania: page 28; Courtesy Library of Congress Prints and Photographs Division: pages 5, 6, 7, 8, 9, 10, 13, 14, 15, 16, 17, 18, 19, 20, 21, 22, 24, 25, 26, 30, 32, 33, 34, 35, 37, 39; Courtesy NASA: page 28; Courtesy National Archives and Records Administration: page 40; Courtesy National Oceanic and Atmospheric Administration: page 11; Courtesy National Parks Service: pages 23, 43; Courtesy Rohm Padilla: pages 4, 29, 38; Courtesy Charles Reasoner: pages 12, 27; Courtesy U.S. Fish and Wildlife Service: Title Page, page 14.

SPECIAL NOTE: Further information about people's names shown in the text in bold can be found on pages 45 and 46. More information about glossary terms in bold can be found on pages 46 and 47.

DESIGN: ROHM PADILLA
LAYOUT/PRODUCTION: LUCY PADILLA

Library of Congress Cataloging-in-Publication Data

Thompson, Linda, 1941-
  The first settlements / Linda Thompson.
     p. cm. -- (Expansion of America II)
  Includes index.
  ISBN 1-59515-511-2 (hardcover)
  1. United States--History--Colonial period, ca. 1600-1775--Juvenile literature. 2. America--Discovery and exploration--European--Juvenile literature. I. Title.
  E188.T47 2006
  973.2--dc22

                                        2005010999

TITLE PAGE IMAGE
Chincoteague National Wildlife Refuge, on the east coast of Virginia

Printed in the USA

TABLE OF CONTENTS

Chapter I
THE NEW WORLD
4

Chapter II
FINS, FURS, AND COLONISTS
14

Chapter III
ROANOKE AND JAMESTOWN
23

Chapter IV
THE PURITANS
32

Chapter V
PLANTING THE SEEDS OF DEMOCRACY
39

A Timeline of the History of the First Settlements
43
Key People
45
Glossary
46
Index
48
Books of Interest
48
Web Sites
48

Only 20 years after it became independent, the United States doubled in size, thanks to President Thomas Jefferson's wise purchase of Louisiana Territory from France. Within 50 years, the

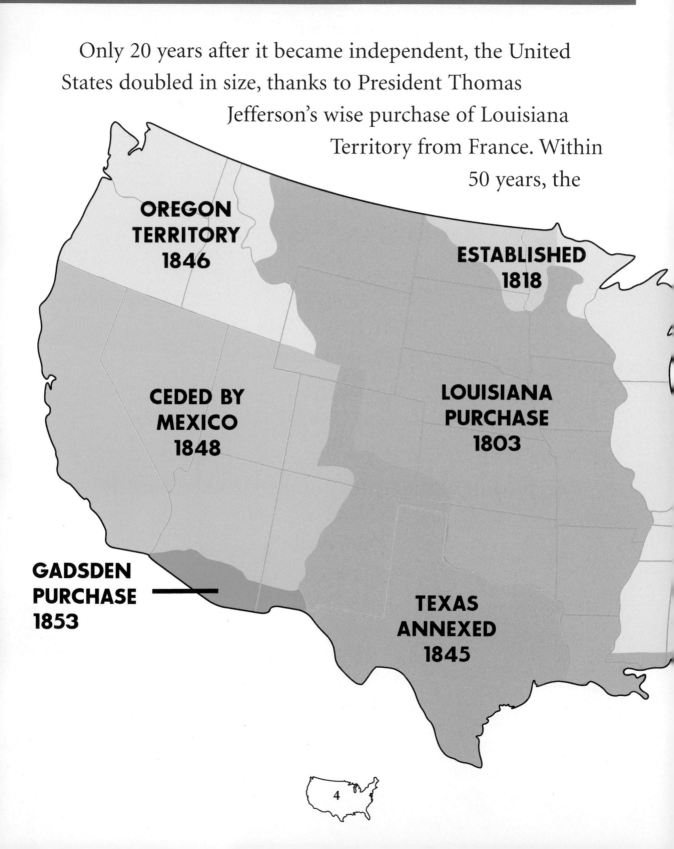

OREGON
TERRITORY
1846

ESTABLISHED
1818

CEDED BY
MEXICO
1848

LOUISIANA
PURCHASE
1803

GADSDEN
PURCHASE ——
1853

TEXAS
ANNEXED
1845

country stretched across immense plains and towering mountain ranges to touch the Pacific Ocean.

How the United States grew so fast in such a short time is an amazing tale. But the expansion that took place after the American Revolution was only a logical continuation of the westbound movement Europeans had begun in 1492 with **Christopher Columbus**. Before that date America had had a few visitors, but they did not bring permanent settlers. The voyages of Columbus were a milestone in American history because they eventually brought great **hordes** of people from across the sea. And once religious and political leaders decided a region might be worthy of settlement, families began to arrive.

UNITED STATES PRIOR TO 1803

CEDED BY SPAIN 1819

Christopher Columbus

5

THE VIKINGS

More than 500 years before Columbus, **Norse** (Scandinavian) seamen known as **Vikings** had sailed to the coast of North America.

Leif Eriksson spies the New World.

One of them, **Leif Eriksson**, landed in 1000 on the coast of what is probably Newfoundland and called it "Vinland." His followers tried to live there, but constant battles with Native Americans made them give up after a few years.

However, the first European explorers of the "New World" were not looking for new places for people to live. The sailors who arrived from Spain, France, England, Portugal, and other countries were actually seeking a sea route to the Orient. India, China, Indonesia (the "Spice Islands"), and their neighbors produced highly desirable goods such as silks, jewelry, and spices. The Italian adventurer, **Marco Polo**, had helped introduce these lands and their products to Europe in the 13th century. But the routes Marco Polo pioneered, leading eastward, were often blocked by hostile forces or controlled by groups that demanded high **taxes**.

6

For the first time, Europeans were building ships that were large and seaworthy enough to sail into the uncharted waters to the west. Christopher Columbus, an Italian whose voyage was paid for by Spain, was one of the first explorers to try to reach the Orient by sailing west. In 1492, he landed on an island in what is now the Bahamas. Thinking it was India, he called the native people he encountered "Indians." Columbus made several more voyages, the last in 1502-03, visiting present-day **Hispaniola**, Cuba (which he thought was Japan), and Jamaica. He died in Spain in 1506, still believing he had reached the Far East.

Christopher Columbus landing in America

One of Columbus's goals had been to find precious metal because the queen of Spain had promised him 10 percent of all he could bring back. Some of the natives he met wore tiny gold ornaments in their ears. In the rivers of Hispaniola, the sailors saw small amounts of gold. When Columbus returned to Spain, he exaggerated, writing that he had seen "…many wide rivers of which the majority contain gold." On his next voyage, finding no gold, he took many Indian slaves instead. Some were sent by ship to Spain but they did not survive the voyage.

Natives presenting gifts to Christopher Columbus and his crew

8

The Spaniards forced hundreds of slaves to work in mines in Hispaniola (which yielded a little gold after a great deal of digging) or in agricultural fields. The Spaniards were harsh masters, and within two years only half of the native population of about 250,000 remained.

A gold nugget

PONCE DE LEON SPOTS U.S. MAINLAND

The first European to sight the mainland of the North American continent was Spanish explorer **Juan Ponce de León** on March 27, 1513. He named the land "La Florida," or "Land of Flowers" in Spanish. For the next 50 years, Spain tried unsuccessfully to establish a colony in Florida.

Juan Ponce de León

This pattern tended to be repeated again and again during the next 50 years, during which Spain conquered Mexico, Peru, and Central America, and Portugal claimed Brazil. The invaders' main goal was to find gold, and their second goal was to convert native people to Christianity. Unfortunately, however, every landing of the Europeans who followed Columbus had severely harmful effects on the millions of people who had occupied America before 1492.

ST. AUGUSTINE

The oldest permanent European settlement in the United States is St. Augustine, Florida, founded in 1565. The Spanish king, **Felipe II**, sent Admiral **Pedro Menendez de Aviles** to build a fort on Florida's shores and keep France out.

Ruins of the fort at St. Augustine, Florida

Menendez destroyed a French garrison on the St. Johns River. He then built a town that for nearly 200 years was home to Spaniards, Indians, Africans, and mixed-blood residents. In 1763, Spain traded Florida to England for Cuba, and St. Augustine became an English colony.

A Spanish explorer proclaims to natives that they are now subjects of the king and must become Christians.

11

In Europe, in the early 16th century, Spain, Portugal, England, France, and the Netherlands had major naval forces. Competition to colonize the New World and harvest its treasures increased rapidly. In 1588, the English brought Spain's domination of the Atlantic Ocean to a standstill by defeating Spain's "invincible **armada**" or fleet of warships. From then on, ships from other countries were free to come and go, and settlement of America could begin **in earnest**. One result would be the rise of colonial territories with names such as "New England," "New Amsterdam," and "New France."

Ships of the Spanish Armada

DISCOVERY OF NORTH AMERICA, BY JOHN AND SEBASTIAN CABOT.

John Cabot planting the English flag in Canada

JOHN CABOT CLAIMS CANADA FOR ENGLAND

In 1497 an Italian explorer, Giovanni Caboto, sailed along the eastern shores of Canada. Known to the English as **John Cabot**, he was seeking a trade route to the Orient for Henry VII of England. The following year, Cabot explored the Atlantic coast from Baffin Island, Canada, to Maryland. These voyages gave England a claim to the northeast coast of North America.

Chapter II: **FINS, FURS, AND COLONISTS**

The gradual realization that Columbus had not reached the Orient was not as disappointing to the seafaring nations as it might have been, for two reasons. First, rumors were spreading about rich cargoes of gold and silver that Spanish treasure ships were now bringing back from the **West Indies**. Secondly, explorers reported that fishing in the waters off North America was excellent!

River otters (above) were one source of furs.
Jacques Cartier's fleet on the St. Lawrence (left)

NEW FRANCE

Sixteenth-century adventurers continued to search for a legendary "great river" through North America that would serve as a short cut to the Far East. In 1524, France sent a navigator from Italy, **Giovanni da Verrazano**, to explore the coastline from Newfoundland in Canada to North Carolina. This gave France a claim to that area. Ten years later, **Jacques Cartier** sailed up the St. Lawrence River to the future **Quebec** and **Montreal**. France's main interest at the time was fish and animal skins. It did not try to establish colonies but sent annual fishing fleets to the waters off Canada. By the early 1600s France had also developed a very profitable fur trade.

Jacques Cartier with natives at Hochelaga, now Montreal

Samuel de
Champlain

In 1608, French navigator **Samuel de Champlain** founded a trading post at Quebec, the first permanent European settlement in Canada. Only 9 of the original 32 colonists survived the harsh winter, but more settlers arrived the following summer. Champlain explored much of the eastern coast as far south as Cape Cod. In 1613 and 1615, he sailed up the St. Lawrence River, eventually reaching Lake Huron and Lake Ontario.

Champlain, who is considered the "father of New France," discouraged farmers from settling but welcomed Catholic missionaries to help convert Native-American allies to Christianity. Within a few **decades**, a dozen missions could be found in the backwoods of New France.

By the end of the 17th century, **René-Robert Cavelier, Sieur de La Salle**, had also claimed the entire Mississippi River **watershed** and the future site of New Orleans, Louisiana, for France. But the scant population of New France and its emphasis on hunting and fishing—instead of farming and making trade goods—meant that France would never be able to use the great river for commercial shipping or defend it when necessary.

NEW NETHERLAND

New York City, which today leads American cities in population, was originally a Dutch settlement! In 1610, English navigator **Henry Hudson**, working for the Dutch East India Company, sailed into the mouth of a river that was later named after him—the Hudson River. He traveled as far north as present-day Albany, New York, and claimed the entire Hudson River valley for the Dutch. In 1614, the New Netherlands Company of Amsterdam built the first Dutch settlement, a small trading post called Fort Nassau, on an island in the Hudson River. It was abandoned in 1617 because of frequent floods. A few years later, Fort Orange (now Albany) was built on the west side of the river. Like the French, the Dutch focused heavily on fur trading and less on farming.

Henry Hudson's ships enter New York harbor.

17

THE DUTCH TRADE IN SLAVES

The Dutch brought the first slave ship to the North American continent when it landed at Jamestown in 1619. At first black Africans were listed as "servants," but they were bought, sold, and treated as slaves. From 1500 to 1800, 12 million African slaves came to the New World, but only about a half million were shipped to the North American colonies. About six million were sent to Central and South America and about five million to the West Indies.

Captives in an African village being sent into slavery

The East India Company had successfully traded with Indonesia and other Far East countries. In 1621 the Netherlands formed the West India Company to conduct business in Africa and North America. It sent 30 Dutch families to Hudson Bay in 1626, and they

Dutch men offering a trade to Native Americans

settled on what is now **Manhattan** Island. This village, Fort Amsterdam, would become the capital of the Dutch colony. By 1630, about 300 people lived there.

In 1626, a director of the West India Company, **Peter Minuit**, arrived to administer the struggling colony. In one of the most amazing bargains of history, he traded 60 guilders worth of cloth, kettles, hatchets, and other goods to a group of Delaware Indians for the island of Manhattan. This was nearly 34 square miles (88 sq km) of valuable land! Although the U.S. dollar had not yet been created, the price is often said to have equaled about 24 dollars. The Indians who "sold" Manhattan lived elsewhere, and since Native Americans had no concept of buying or selling land they may have thought they were merely selling hunting rights. In any case, the Dutch ended up with Manhattan and named it "New Amsterdam."

WALL STREET

Peter Stuyvesant tried to ward off the inevitable English invasion of New Amsterdam in 1653. The city was at the southern tip of the island, and the Dutch decided to build a wall across the north end. Made of 12-foot-high (3.6-meter) logs, it stretched for half a mile across the island. No English attack came that year, but the wall remained and a street near it was named **Wall Street**.

In 1729, the first **stock exchange** office opened at 22 Wall Street and the name took on a meaning that remains world famous today.

Peter Stuyvesant (above). Wall Street in New York (below) in 1847

As settlements grew, the Dutch colonists found Native Americans to be in the way and carried out harsh campaigns against them. Also, the Dutch created ill will by taking over Fort

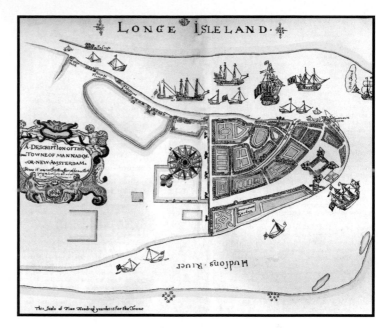

Map of Manhattan, 1661

Cristina (near present-day Wilmington, Delaware), a Swedish colony of about 500 people that had begun in 1638. The new Dutch director, Peter Stuyvesant [sty-va-sant] considered "New Sweden" a threat to commerce and **annexed** the colony without a fight in 1655. But in less than 10 years, the tables had turned. In 1664 Stuyvesant was forced to surrender New Netherland with its 9,000 colonists to the English!

England had many reasons to declare war on Holland, including colonial interests and competition for African slaves and ivory. Both countries were eager to dominate the seas, along with the wealth now flowing to Europe from far-away lands. So **Charles II**, king of England, decided to give a gift— New Netherland—to his 30-year-old brother, **James Stuart**, **Duke of York**! All King Charles had to do was go get it.

William Penn negotiates with Native Americans and founds Pennsylvania.

Charles II sent four **frigates** to New Amsterdam, and Stuyvesant surrendered without a fight since he had no navy and Holland did not show up to defend the colony. Charles's gift to his brother consisted of the present state of New York, along with land that now makes up parts of Maine, Connecticut, Pennsylvania, New Jersey, and Delaware. The English renamed New Amsterdam "New York," and gave the entire province the same name. The Duke gave New Jersey to two of his friends. Then he gave another young settler, **William Penn**, a large piece of land that later became the state of Pennsylvania.

Chapter III: ROANOKE AND JAMESTOWN

English writers and promoters tried to lure people to America in the early 1600s. For example, a poem about "Virginia" by Michael Drayton was widely published:

Virginia, Earth's only paradise.
Where Nature hath in store Fowle, Venison and Fish,
And the Fruitfull'st Soyle, without your Toyle,
Three harvests more, all greater than your Wish,
And the ambitious Vine, crownes with his purple Masse,
The cedar reaching hie to kisse the Sky,
The Cypresse, Pine and use-full Sassafras.

Mountains of Virginia

English settlers bound for America

Of course, the reality of the New World—a treacherous sea crossing, difficult weather, harsh soil conditions, and native people who resisted foreigners—did not exactly add up to a paradise. Most people who left London were sailors, **bachelors**, adventurers, farmers, the unemployed, and some **convicts**.

WHY DID ENGLAND ENCOURAGE EMIGRATION?

England was considered overpopulated, with limited chances for all but the upper class. One solution was to talk poorer folks into sailing for America. Also, merchants hoped to sell woolen goods in parts of North America with a cold climate and to grow olive trees and grapes where the climate was warm. England had a religious interest as well—it wanted to limit the influence of Catholic countries such as Spain and France in the New World. Finally, England hoped that large amounts of gold and silver similar to those found in Peru and Mexico might exist in North America.

The first English attempt at a colony in the New World happened even before 1600. In 1585 **Sir Walter Raleigh** sent about a hundred men to Roanoke Island in "Virginia," off the coast of what is now North Carolina. "Virginia" was a poorly defined land, larger than it

Sir Walter Raleigh

is today. Raleigh and others had named it in honor of England's "Virgin Queen," **Elizabeth I**. A year later **Sir Francis Drake**, a "**sea dog**" returning from a raid on Spanish ships in the West Indies, stopped at Roanoke. He found the remaining colonists ready to give up. Many had been killed by natives or died of hunger or diseases such as **malaria** and **dysentery**. Drake took the survivors back to England and another ship left 15 men at the colony to defend it.

Sir Francis Drake

SEA DOGS

In the mid-16th century, a number of "sea dogs"—men who combined fighting with sailing, adventure, and trade—became famous in England. Among them were Francis Drake and Walter Raleigh. Eventually, many of the sea dogs were knighted by the queen of England and afterward were called "Sir."

But Raleigh was determined and sent about 120 settlers, including 17 women, to Roanoke in three ships in 1587. Their leader was Captain **John White**, whose daughter, Elenora, and her husband were also on board. Within a few months, they had a child and named her **Virginia Dare**. She was the first English child born in America. As for the 15 men, only some bones were found to hint at their fate. Nevertheless, the new settlers rebuilt the houses, planted crops, and prepared to stay.

Unfortunately, Raleigh's timing was bad because England was at war with Spain and needed all of its resources to defeat the Spanish armada. England neglected the colony until 1590, when more ships arrived at Roanoke. Not a single person could be found.

Only some armor, maps, rusting iron, and the ruins of
structures remained, along with
the word "Croatoan" carved
on a tree. The sailors guessed
that any survivors had headed
toward Croatoan Island, 100
miles (160 km) south of
the Carolinas. Today,
their fate remains a
mystery. Sir Walter
Raleigh was said
to have lost
40,000 English
pounds (about $4
million in today's
money) on the
ill-fated settlement of
Roanoke.

Elenora and
Virginia Dare

Remnants of a church tower from the Jamestown settlement (above). Chesapeake Bay, with the James River indicated in red (below).

CHESAPEAKE BAY

JAMESTOWN

Sixteen years passed before England was ready to try again. On December 20, 1606, three small ships—the *Susan Constant, Godspeed,* and *Discovery*—sailed from London. People were crowded onto these ships, which were sponsored by the Virginia Company of London. After four rough months at sea, they came to **Chesapeake Bay**, on the Atlantic coast of present-day Virginia. The ships sailed about 60 miles (97 km) up a river that flowed into Chesapeake Bay. The voyagers named it James River after King James I of England. They pitched tents and called their settlement Jamestown. It became the first permanent English settlement in the New World.

Just like the Roanoke pioneers, the colonists of Jamestown experienced major difficulties. Of the 144 people who sailed from England, only 105 arrived alive. They **disembarked** on May 14, 1607, and 12 days later faced their first battle with natives. They made the mistake of building their fortress, church, and houses in a low,

John Smith

swampy area, and many became ill. In addition to disease, they contended with hunger and exhausting work. Captain **John Smith**, the colony's first leader, was strict about everybody doing his share. He said, "He that will not work, neither will he eat." After less than two years, only 60 people were still alive.

COLONIZATION AS AN INVESTMENT

Like other countries, England lacked resources to establish and maintain colonies. The royalty granted private companies **charters** to form settlements, first in Virginia and later in New England. The investors' main interest was trading furs and skins. Investors paid the costs of establishing a colony by buying stock in the company at 12 pounds (about $62 in gold) per share.

The survivors were about to abandon Jamestown when a new ship arrived carrying several hundred men and a new leader, **Lord de la Warr**. Both he and his successor, Sir Thomas Dale, imposed strict military discipline. The colonists had no hope of owning land because they were working for the benefit of London stockholders. By 1612, their only cash crop was cedar wood. However, in 1613, a new crop came along that would change the colony's destiny—tobacco.

As the wife of John Rolfe, Pocahantas visited the court of King James.

One Jamestown colonist, **John Rolfe**, is famous for two things—he saved Jamestown by introducing tobacco, and he married a young **Powhatan** woman named **Pocahontas**. Rolfe brought seeds of a mild strain of tobacco from the West Indies, crossed them with native tobacco seeds, and produced a new variety. Virginia tobacco became instantly popular with English traders, storekeepers, and consumers. By 1618, Virginia was exporting 50,000 pounds (22,700 kg) of tobacco a year to England. Although King James stated that tobacco was unhealthy, he did not prohibit its import. The Virginia Company convinced the English **Parliament** that only tobacco could save Jamestown from disaster.

Jamestown's success was also helped by a legal change that allowed colonists to acquire land. After working for seven years, a man could become a **tenant farmer**. After another 10 years or so, the land he worked became his. Hundreds of field laborers took advantage of this opportunity and became plantation owners. In addition, more women began to join the colony. The Virginia Company would send an unmarried woman to any planter who wanted a wife in return for 150 pounds (68 kg) of prime tobacco. The creation of families gave the settlers more reason to stay.

During the 16th century England began having religious conflicts as part of a movement throughout the Christian world called the **Reformation**. Some people criticized official church doctrine and wanted to separate completely from it. They called themselves "**Puritans**" because they wanted a "pure," or direct link between each individual and God— without rituals, saints, popes, and other **intermediaries**.

Puritans on their way to church

32

In 1608 some English Puritans fled to Leyden, Holland, and were granted **asylum**. In 1620 a group of these Leyden Puritans led by **William Brewster** received a **land grant** from the Virginia Company, which allowed them to join others who were leaving for America. They agreed to be **indentured servants** to London investors for a number of years.

On September 16, 1620, 102 men, women, and children set sail from Plymouth, England, heading for Virginia on the *Mayflower*. Fewer than half were Puritans, while the rest were adventurers or others who desired to leave England. Almost 180 years later, historians named these passengers "The **Pilgrims**."

Mayflower approaching landfall

The Pilgrims sign the Mayflower Compact on board the ship.

A storm blew the ship northward, and on November 19 it landed near present-day Provincetown on Cape Cod. Believing themselves outside the **domain** of both the Virginia Company and the crown, they drafted a formal agreement called the **Mayflower Compact**. They agreed to abide by any "just and equal laws" their government might pass and to have the right to choose their own leaders.

They sailed a bit further, and on December 21 they landed at a spot that Captain John Smith had named Plymouth, on the coast of present-day Massachusetts. During the first winter they lost nearly half of their party to exposure and disease, but they decided to stay. The Native Americans there—the **Wampanoag**—were helpful and taught them to grow **maize** (corn). By the following year, the Pilgrims had a good crop of corn and had harvested furs and lumber to sell. Early leaders of this colony included **John Carver**, **John Alden**, and **William Bradford**, who was the colony's governor for more than 30 years.

Landing at Plymouth Rock

SQUANTO

Pilgrims brought wheat seeds, which would not grow in New England's rocky soil. A member of the Wampanoag named **Tisquantum**, or **Squanto**, taught them how to grow corn. He had traveled to England years before and learned English. Some months after the Pilgrims arrived, Squanto and his friend, **Samoset**, startled the newcomers by saying "Welcome" in English. Squanto stayed with the Pilgrims for a few months, bringing them deer meat and beaver skins. He taught them about the local plants, how to dig clams and use fish for fertilizer, and hundreds of other survival skills.

Squanto helping a settler

The colonies might not have grown had it not been for a great religious **emigration** from England in the 1630s. About one thousand immigrants, mostly Puritans, arrived in 15 ships in 1630. Led by **John Winthrop**, they had a grant from Charles I to establish the **Massachusetts Bay Colony**, first at present-day Salem, Massachusetts,

Plaque set in remembrance of the founding of the Massachusetts Bay Colony

and later at Boston. By the mid-1600s more than 15,000 Puritans had left England for America, seeking religious and economic opportunities.

The Puritans maintained friendships with merchants in England, who supplied them with **credit** to buy supplies. In return, they produced dried fish, cattle, and corn. When English support faded in 1637 because of political troubles, the settlers became more self-sufficient. They began a shipbuilding industry and sold products such as salted beef and dried fish to the West Indies, using the money to buy supplies in England. This trade sustained New England for many years. In 1684 the Massachusetts Bay Colony came under direct British rule and in 1691 merged with Plymouth and Maine (then a part of Massachusetts).

After the initial success of these settlements, other English colonies quickly formed. In 1632, **Lord Baltimore** founded Maryland (later called Baltimore) for Roman Catholics. In 1636, **Roger Williams** and **Anne Hutchinson** were expelled from Massachusetts for being too liberal. They and a few others founded Rhode Island. In 1639, New Haven (the future Connecticut) was formed.

By the mid-17th century, small groups of settlers were also living in the present states of New Hampshire and North Carolina. A South Carolina settlement founded in 1670 became Charles Towne in 1680 after King Charles II. This is now Charleston, South Carolina. By 1733, the 13 original colonies were in place, making up the core of what would become the United States of America.

Orange indicates the area of the original 13 colonies.

Chapter V: PLANTING THE SEEDS OF DEMOCRACY

In Jamestown, in July 1619, the first meeting of a representative government was held in America. To encourage the struggling colonists to stay, the Virginia Company permitted a certain degree of self-rule. The **House of Burgesses** was the result. It may seem limited compared with what Americans enjoy today, but even this much self-governance was unheard of in the European colonies. The company appointed a governor, who then selected a council of six. Fifteen burgesses, representatives from different districts, made up the rest of the general assembly. At first they were landowners from the larger plantations. Only free men more than 17 years old could vote for the burgesses.

A speech in the House of Burgesses

The Bill of Rights, from the U.S. Constitution

The Massachusetts colony also took important steps toward democracy. It developed a statement of individual rights that became the basis for the **Bill of Rights** in the U.S. Constitution. The Plymouth Colony's "**General Fundamentals**" called for annual elections and specified that anyone accused of a crime must be tried by a **jury**. Also, no colonists would be taxed without being represented in the government. The Massachusetts "**Body of Liberties**," adopted in 1641, also said that people should not have to **incriminate** themselves and that nobody would be deprived of life, liberty, or property except by due process of law.

These American "seeds of democracy" grew out of England's promises to the colonists combined with the straightforward forms of religion these emigrants brought with them. The first charter of the Virginia Company in 1606 assured colonists and their descendants "all liberties…

as if they had been abiding and born within this our realm of England." One such liberty was trial by jury and another was having some say over taxation. The colonists eventually expanded on these freedoms to create a more democratic form of government than any that existed in Europe or England at the time.

Free education is one of New England's lasting contributions to the United States. By 1642, parents were required to teach their children to read and write. By 1647 every settlement with more than 50 families had to appoint a schoolmaster, who taught Latin and Greek grammar and literature as well as **arithmetic**. Four of these early schools—Boston Latin, Cambridge Latin, Roxbury Latin, and Hopkins Grammar School of New Haven—still exist today as high schools.

In 1636 the Massachusetts Bay Colony set up a college named after Reverend **John Harvard**, which in 1650 became chartered as Harvard College. Its purpose was "the advancement of all good literature, arts and sciences." Students sometimes paid their tuition with produce, clothing, or live cattle. More than half of Harvard graduates in the 17th century became ministers. Today that college is Harvard University.

The people who sailed for America tended to be "rugged individualists" who expected to find themselves in an uncivilized wilderness without laws, institutions, or even support from their parent country. They were prepared to form their own government and laws. Also, because they had to depend upon each other for survival, they were generally inclined to treat people as equals. Because of their need to be self-reliant, they were open to change.

The Puritans brought with them an intense desire for religious freedom. Yet, most of the colonies did not practice it themselves. The idea of **tolerating** other systems of belief was **radical**. Of all New England's founders, only Roger Williams, Lord Baltimore, and William Penn publicly called for religious tolerance. Later, however, in the 18th century, there were so many different churches that tolerance began to be more accepted.

From the dawn of European exploration, the New World was a place where many different cultures competed and clashed with one another. Settlement attempts sometimes succeeded and often failed, but one thing was true. As early settlers moved on and more European immigrants arrived, the country's growth advanced steadily in one direction—westward toward the setting sun.

Sun setting over the mountains of Virginia

A Timeline of the History of *The First Settlements*

CE 1000	Leif Eriksson sails to the coast of what is probably Newfoundland and calls it "Vinland."
1492	Christopher Columbus lands on an island in what is now the Bahamas, believing it to be India.
1497	Giovanni Caboto, or John Cabot, sails along the eastern shores of Canada, giving England a claim to North America.
1513	Spanish explorer Juan Ponce de León sights the North American continent and calls it "Florida."
1524	France sends Giovanni da Verrazano to explore the coastline of present-day Canada, establishing a French claim to North America.
1565	The oldest permanent European settlement in the United States is founded at St. Augustine, Florida.
1585-1587	Sir Walter Raleigh tries to colonize Roanoke Island in "Virginia."
1588	England defeats Spain's "invincible armada."
1590	Rescuers find that all Roanoke colonists have vanished.
1598	Jacques Cartier explores the St. Lawrence River to the future sites of Quebec and Montreal.

1607	The *Susan Constant, Godspeed,* and *Discovery* bring the first colonists to Jamestown.
1608	French navigator Samuel de Champlain founds a trading post at Quebec.
1610	Santa Fe, New Mexico, the oldest capital city in the United States, is founded by Spain. Henry Hudson sails into Hudson Bay and up the Hudson River, claiming it for the Dutch East India Company.
1613	John Rolfe saves Jamestown by introducing a new strain of tobacco.
1614	First Dutch settlement, Fort Nassau, near future Albany, New York.
1619	The Dutch bring the first slave ship to the North American continent.
1620	The *Mayflower* arrives at Plymouth in what is now Massachusetts.
1626	First Dutch settlers on what is now Manhattan Island. Peter Minuit buys the island from Native Americans for trade goods worth 60 guilders (about $24 dollars).
1630	The first wave of thousands of new Puritan colonists arrive and the Massachusetts Bay Colony is established.
1655	Peter Stuyvesant annexes "New Sweden."
1664	Stuyvesant surrenders New Netherland to England and it is renamed "New York."
1682	René-Robert Cavelier, Sieur de La Salle claims the entire Mississippi River watershed and the site of New Orleans, Louisiana, for France
1733	All of the 13 original American colonies have taken shape.

Alden, John (1599?-1687) - American settler, signer of the Mayflower Compact and organizer of Plymouth Colony.

Bradford, William (1590-1657) - Colonial governor and signer of the Mayflower Compact. His *History of Plimoth Plantation, 1620-46* is the basis for all accounts of the Plymouth Colony.

Brewster, William (1567-1644) - Pilgrim religious leader, signer of the Mayflower Compact, and leader at Plymouth Colony.

Cabot, John (Giovanni Caboto, 1450?-1498) - Italian-born navigator and explorer employed by Henry VII of England. His explorations gave England claims to America.

Cartier, Jacques (1491-1557) - French explorer of North America.

Carver, John (1576?-1621) - First governor of Plymouth Colony.

Champlain, Samuel de (1567-1635) - French explorer, founder of New France (Canada) and Quebec (1608).

Charles II (1630-1685) - King of England, Scotland, and Ireland (1660-85).

Columbus, Christopher (Cristobal Colón) (1451-1506) - Italian explorer in the service of Spain who discovered America for the Europeans in 1492.

Dare, Virginia (1587-?) - First English child born in America (Roanoke Colony), granddaughter of governor John White, who disappeared with the other colonists by 1590.

De la Warr, Lord Thomas West (1577-1618) - Baron and colonial governor of Jamestown (1610-1611). The state of Delaware is named after him.

Drake, Francis (1540-1596) - English sailor and adventurer ("sea dog") who raided Spanish ships and colonies in the Caribbean.

Elizabeth I (1533-1603) - Queen of England (1558-1603) who reestablished Protestantism. During her reign, England became a major naval power, defeating the Spanish armada.

Eriksson, Leif - Norse explorer, son of Eric the Red, who discovered the North American continent for Europeans about CE 1000.

Felipe II (Philip II, 1527-1598) - King of Spain (1556-96) who ruled one of the great empires of history; his armada was defeated by England in 1588.

Harvard, John (1607-1638) - Young minister who left his library and half of his estate to a college named after him, Harvard College.

Hudson, Henry (died 1611) - English navigator and explorer for whom Hudson Bay and the Hudson River in New York were named.

Hutchinson, Anne (1591?-1643) - English colonist and religious leader. Banned from the Massachusetts Bay Colony for her views, she helped settle Portsmouth, Rhode Island.

La Salle, René-Robert Cavelier, Sieur de (1643-1687) - French explorer in North America. First to explore the Mississippi to its mouth, he claimed the land for Louis XIV of France (1682).

Lord Baltimore (Cecilius Calvert, 1605?-1675) - First proprietor of Maryland, who inherited the charter from his father, George Calvert, who died before the charter was issued.

Menendez de Aviles, Pedro (1519-1574) - Spanish explorer who established the settlement of St. Augustine, Florida (1565). He became Florida's first Spanish governor.

Minuit, Peter (1580-1638) - First governor of New Netherland, purchased Manhattan Island from the Indians (1620).

Penn, William (1644-1718) - Founder of Pennsylvania, became a Quaker in 1666 and was imprisoned several times for his religious views. Designer of the city of Philadelphia.

Pocahontas (1595-1617) - Daughter of Powhatan chief (Powhatan) and wife of Jamestown settler, John Rolfe.

Polo, Marco (1254?-1324) - First European to cross the length of Asia, he gave the first account of China and the Far East in his report, *The Description of the World* (1295).

Ponce de León, Juan (1460?-1521) - Spanish explorer who traveled with Columbus on his second voyage. Served as governor of Puerto

Rico (1510-12) and explored the Florida coast (1513).

Raleigh, Walter (1552?-1618) - English soldier and "sea dog," knighted by Queen Elizabeth I in 1585. Wrote *History of the World*, 1614.

Rolfe, John (1585-1622) - English colonist, the first to cultivate tobacco in Jamestown.

Samoset - A Mohegan Indian who knew some English and greeted the Pilgrims by saying "Welcome."

Smith, John (1580-1631) - English soldier and colonial leader, first head of the Jamestown colony; explored the New England coast and gave the region its name.

Squanto (Tisquantum) (died 1622) - Pawtuxet Indian of Massachusetts, acted as interpreter for the Pilgrims of Plymouth Colony and helped them learn to survive.

Stuart, James, Duke of York (King James II of England) (1633-1701) - He succeeded his brother Charles II as king in 1685. New York was named after him.

Stuyvesant, Peter (1610?-1672) - Dutch colonial governor. Became director of New Netherland in 1647.

Verrazano, Giovanni da (1480?-1527) - Italian explorer in the service of France, first to explore the Hudson River and Manhattan Island.

White, John (1537?-1600?) - Sir Walter Raleigh's surveyor-general in Virginia and later governor of Roanoke (1587-1590).

Williams, Roger (1603-1683) - Advocate of religious freedom and founder of Rhode Island.

Winthrop, John (1588-1649) - Governor of the Massachusetts Bay Colony. Served as president of the New England Confederation and wrote *History of New England 1630-49*.

GLOSSARY

annex - To add to something earlier, larger, or more important; to attach.

arithmetic - The part of mathematics that deals with adding, subtracting, multiplying, and dividing.

armada - From Spanish, "armed"; a fleet of warships.

asylum - A place of shelter and protection.

bachelor - An unmarried man.

Bill of Rights - The first 10 amendments to the U.S. Constitution.

Body of Liberties - A group of laws passed by the Massachusetts Bay Colony in 1641 dealing with personal rights.

charter - A grant or guarantee from a state or country.

Chesapeake Bay - Inlet of the Atlantic Ocean into Virginia and Maryland at the mouth of the Susquehanna River.

convict - A person who has been found guilty of a crime and (usually) is serving or has served a sentence for it.

credit - An amount placed at a person's disposal by a bank or other lender.

decade - A period of 10 years.

disembark - To go ashore from a ship.

domain - A territory or area over which some ownership, power, or influence is held.

dysentery - A disease marked by diarrhea and usually caused by infection.

emigration - The movement of a person or group away from a place or country.

frigate - A light boat driven by sails; a small warship.

General Fundamentals - A group of laws passed by the Plymouth Colony that specified some of the individual rights later incorporated into the U.S. Bill of Rights.

Hispaniola - Second largest island in the West Indies, now divided into Haiti (formerly St. Domingue, a French colony) and the Dominican Republic.

horde - A crowd or swarm.

House of Burgesses - Branch of the legislature of colonial Virginia that allowed colonists to have a say in how they were governed.

in earnest - Having a determined and serious state of mind; sincere.

incriminate - To charge with a crime or show proof of involvement in a crime or fault.

indentured servant - A person who commits to work for another for a specified period in return for favors such as travel expenses and possibly room and board.

intermediary - A go-between or agent.

jury - A body of persons sworn to give a verdict according to the evidence presented.

land grant - A transfer of land by the government to another party.

maize - Corn.

malaria - A human disease caused by parasites in the red blood cells and spread by the bites of mosquitoes.

Manhattan - An island 13 miles (21 km) long that makes up one part of New York City.

Massachusetts Bay Colony - An early settlement in North America founded with a charter to John Winthrop first at Salem and later at Boston, Massachusetts.

Mayflower - The ship that brought the first Puritans from England to New England in 1620.

Mayflower Compact - An agreement to form a government, signed by the 41 male passengers of the *Mayflower* off the New England coast on November 21, 1620.

Montreal - City in the province of Quebec, Canada, settled in 1642 by the French.

Norse - Relating to ancient Scandinavia or the language spoken there; also, Norwegian.

Parliament - The law-making body of government in England.

Pilgrim - One who journeys in foreign lands; the name later given to the Puritans who first settled New England.

Powhatan - A major group of Native Americans in Virginia; also, the name of the chief who was Pocahontas's father.

Puritan - Member of a religious reform movement that developed in England during the late 16th century.

Quebec - Canada's oldest city and the capital of Quebec province.

radical - Tending to extremes, for example in politics, desiring to make extreme changes in existing views or institutions.

Reformation - A major change in western Christianity that developed between the 14th and 17th centuries. It had to do with moving away from the Roman Catholic Church.

sea dog - A veteran sailor; also, a nickname given to adventurers who made a name for themselves on the seas, often as pirates, in the early 16th century.

stock exchange - A place where ownership shares of companies are bought and sold.

tax - A charge placed by an authority on persons or property to raise money for public purposes.

tenant farmer - A farmer who works land owned by another and pays rent either in cash or in shares of what the farm produces.

tolerate - To put up with, endure.

Treaty of Guadalupe Hidalgo - The agreement that ended the war between the United States and Mexico in 1848.

Viking - One of a group of Scandinavian pirates who roamed the seas in the 10th and 11th centuries.

Wall Street - Site of the New York Stock Exchange.

Wampanoag - A member of a Native American group living in the vicinity of present-day Rhode Island.

watershed - All of the land that drains into a specific body of water, such as a river.

West Indies - The islands lying between southeastern North America and northern South America, just north and east of the Caribbean Sea.

INDEX

Alden, John 35
Baltimore, Lord 38, 42
Bradford, William 35
Brewster, Willliam 33
Cabot, John 13, 43
Canada 13, 15-16
Cartier, Jacques 14-15, 43
Carver, John   35
Champlain, Samuel de 16, 44
Charles I 37
Charles II 21-22
Charles Towne 38
Columbus, Christopher 5, 7-8, 43
Croatoan Island 27
Dale, Thomas 30
Dare, Virginia 26-27
De la Warr, Lord 30
De León, Ponce 9, 43
Drake, Francis 25, 26
Duke of York, James Stuart 21
Elizabeth I 25
Eriksson, Leif 6, 43
Felipe II 11

Harvard, John 41
Hispaniola 7-9
House of Burgesses 39
Hudson, Henry 17, 44
Hutchinson, Anne 38
James I 28, 30-31
Jamestown 23, 28-31, 39, 44
Jefferson, Thomas 4
Manhattan 19, 44
Massachusetts Bay Colony 37, 40-41, 44
Mayflower 33, 44
Menendez de Aviles, Pedro 11
Minuit, Peter 19, 44
Native Americans 6, 7-10, 19, 21, 24, 35, 36
New Amsterdam 12, 19-20, 22
New England 12
New France 12, 16
New Netherland 17, 21, 44
New Sweden 21
New York 17, 22, 44
Penn, William 22, 42
Pilgrims 33-36

Plymouth Colony 35, 37, 40, 44
Pocahontas 30-31
Polo, Marco 6
Puritans 32-33, 37, 42, 44
Raleigh, Walter 25, 26-27, 43
Reformation 32
Roanoke 23, 25-27, 43
Rolfe, John 31
Sieur de La Salle, René Robert Cavelier 16, 44
Smith, John 29, 35
Squanto 36
St. Augustine 11, 43
Stuyvesant, Peter 20-21, 44
Tobacco 30-31, 44
Verrazano, Giovanni da 15, 43
Vikings 6
Virginia Company 28, 31, 33-34, 39, 40
Wall Street 20
White, John 26
Williams, Roger 38, 42
Winthrop, John 37

Books of Interest

Hakim, Joy. *A History of US, Book 2: Making Thirteen Colonies (History of US)*, Oxford University Press, 3rd ed., 2002.

Kimmel, Elizabeth Cody. *Before Columbus: The Leif Eriksson Expedition: A True Adventure (Landmark Books)*, Random House Books for Young Readers, 2003.

Knight, James. *Jamestown*, Scholastic, 2004.

Maestro, Betsy. *Exploration and Conquest : The Americas After Columbus: 1500-1620 (The American Story)*, School & Library Binding, 1999.

Rossi, Ann. *Cultures Collide: Native Americans and Europeans 1492-1700 (Crossroads America)*, National Geographic, 2004.

Web Sites

The history of New Netherland:
http://www.nnp.org/project/index.html

Colonial America links and resources:
http://www.mcps.k12.md.us/schools/travilahes/colonial.html

http://falcon.jmu.edu/~ramseyil/colonial.htm

http://www.kidinfo.com/American_History/Colonization_Colonial_Life.html

---

Linda Thompson is a Montana native and a graduate of the University of Washington. She was a teacher, writer, and editor in the San Francisco Bay Area for 30 years and now lives in Taos, New Mexico. She can be contacted through her web site,

http://www.highmesaproductions.com